A GALLERY OF OUR OWN
HARRIET POWERS
WOMEN OF ART HISTORY

Written and Illustrated
by Melanie Baxter

002000611471

Published by:
Queen MAB Arts
Dallas, TX
www.queenmabarts.com

For Nana, who taught me to love quilts.

Contents

Introduction

Throughout history, women have been excluded and their contributions dismissed. A Gallery of Our Own seeks to balance art history and art appreciation by teaching the artistic contributions of women. There is little information available about women artists. Even when they could make an impact in their own time it was rarely documented, or evidence was later destroyed. This series will teach about the artists, the art movements they were a part of, the history during the time in which they lived, and the forms of art they created. It also includes hands-on projects using a variety of mediums and techniques.

How to Use This Book

Each book in this series can be used as a standalone art curriculum. They will teach art history, appreciation, and techniques. A single book can be used anywhere from 6 weeks to a whole year depending on the speed the student can take in the information, how many parts of each lesson you use with your students, the additional resources used, and how much time you want to devote to art lessons each week.

Lessons

A lesson can be completed in a single session or stretched out over many sessions. It is unnecessary to do all the activities. Included are a variety of activities to work for all levels or mixed age groups. Pick what works for your students. There are links to optional videos for visual learners. It is important that lessons be fun and within the student's ability. The goal is to enjoy art, not perceive it as a chore to rush through.

Preschoolers may:

1. Listen to only part of the informational text (or listen to a picture book instead)
2. Make verbal observations about the art
3. Do the Art in Action section
4. Freely explore the art materials

Elementary students may:

1. Listen to the included text
2. Dictate their observations to an adult to journal for later reference
3. Verbally answer the vocabulary questions
4. Do the Art in Action section
5. Do the art project

Middle school students may:

1. Listen to or read the text
2. Fill in the journal on their own
3. Answer all the questions
4. Do a more involved art project than the elementary students
5. Have an art show with friends and family or at the public library, or give a presentation on what they have learned

High school students may:

1. Read the text
2. Create their own hand-drawn journal with sketches of the artworks they observe
3. Do a comparison with other artists or movements
4. Write an article about the artist as though they are a contemporary
5. Do large, long-term projects with higher quality materials
6. Have an art show with friends and family or at the public library, or give a presentation on what they have learned

Time to Create

Younger students will focus on exploration of the materials and the process of creating. Teaching children to care for their art materials from the beginning is very important. Even the youngest children can learn to respect the materials. Paint in the direction of the bristles and do not scrub to preserve the brushes. Rinse brushes thoroughly and blot on a towel between colors, then wash and hang with bristles down to dry after each session (storing wet brushes with the bristles up can cause the wood to swell or rot and the brushes to fall apart). Paint mixing should be done on a pallet or plate, not directly in the paint jar (but don't discourage mixing, even when the mess is hard to bear). Keep yarn tidy, etc.

When the students are creating art, don't critique or point out flaws. Encourage them to put forth their best effort and complete the project, but their creations are their own and should be done the way they choose. When praising art, point out specifics (these colors make the painting look happy, your person looks just like so-and-so, I love the way these shapes work together). Specific praise shows you are really paying attention and looking closely at their art, and they will notice the difference.

Copyright and Printing

Make as many copies of the journal pages as you need for your family or class, as long as you don't sell them or share them without credit.

Lesson 1

Harriet's Early Life

United States

Georgia

Harriet Angeline Powers was born enslaved on October 29th, 1837. She was born in Madison County Georgia. Her maiden name is unknown. She lived in Clark County near Athens, Georgia for more than half of her life.

Clark County

Georgia

She learned to read at 11 years old. The white children showed her the letters on poplar leaves. After learning to read, she studied books on her own.

Harriet married Armstead Powers in 1855, she was only 18 years old. They had 9 children. They named the 3 surviving children Amanda, Leon Joe, and Nancy.

When Harriet and her family were free, they moved to Dondy, Georgia. There she made a quilt she described as 4050 diamonds in 1872. After becoming a member of Mount Zion Baptist Church in 1882, she created a quilt of the Lord's Supper she described as 2500 diamonds. The family moved to Athens, Georgia in 1886. In 1887 she entered her star quilt in a fair and won a prize. The whereabouts of these quilts are unknown.

Slavery

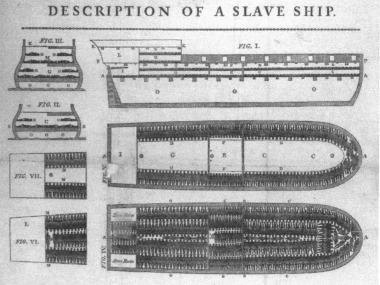

European colonists kidnapped and bought people on the continent of Africa and brought them to the colonies, packed tightly on ships. Many people died during the trip because of the horrible conditions: no room to lie down, disease, starvation, and abuse.

Once in the Americas, the enslaved people were sold to plantation owners and forced to work. They were provided very little food, clothing, or shelter and were often beaten and worked in harsh conditions.

Oak Alley Plantation in Vacherie, Louisiana.

Families were split up and sold to different plantations. When enslaved people tried to escape, they were hunted down and brought back, facing harsh consequences on their return. The Underground Railroad was a secret route of safe houses and helpful people that helped enslaved people escape to freedom.

Slave Quarters in Charleston, SC

Harriet Tubman, born enslaved and escaped in 1849, was an amazing woman. She returned at least 13 times to free hundreds of other enslaved people as a "conductor" on the Underground Railroad. She also worked as a spy for the Union Army during the Civil War.

During the Civil War, the Emancipation Proclamation declared all enslaved people free. Not all enslaved people were freed right away, though. After the Civil War, the 13th Amendment outlawed slavery.

A carte-de-visite of a young Harriet Tubman seated in an interior room. Photographed by Benjamin F. Powelson in 1868-69. Originally owned by Emily Howland, a Quaker schoolteacher who worked in Arlington, VA. Jointly purchased by the National Museum of African American History and Culture and the Library of Congress in 2017.

Examining the Artwork

Spend some time examining the work. Have the children write or tell you 5 things they notice about the artwork (optional journal pages are found at the end of the book). If they get stuck, try asking: What is going on? What do you see that makes you think that? What more can you find? Try not to ask questions that are too specific or give them any answers, let the observations be their own. Experience creates more lasting memories. It may take a while before they can look closely and come up with observations on their own, or are comfortable sharing them. After they have made their own observations, you can use the optional vocabulary and discussion questions below to look deeper.

Vocabulary

1. Contrast- using the differences in elements (rough/smooth, big/small, light/dark, etc.) to make a piece interesting.
   Where is contrast used in this piece? What does it do for the figures?
2. Line- a mark showing the path of a moving point. Lines can be curved, straight, vertical, horizontal, diagonal, zigzagged, curly, dotted, dashed, crisscrossed, thick, thin, etc.
   What kinds of lines did the artist use in this quilt?
3. Proportion- how the element sizes relate to each other.
   Do the forms look proportionate to each other?
4. Storyteller- someone who tells stories, orally or visually.
5. Oral Traditions- knowledge is passed from one generation to another by telling stories or singing.

Art in Action

Describe the artwork to each other using only your bodies and gestures (pantomime).
What was happening in history when this artwork was made? How does that change your understanding of the artwork?

Time To Create: Tell a Story

Materials:

- Storyboard template from the journal in the back of this book (you will only need 1, choose the layout you like for your quilt)
- Pencil

Harriet Powers portrayed familiar bible stories and astrological events in her quilts. Write a story of your own that you will illustrate in the next lesson. Think about how you can tell the story with simple pictures using the templates in the journal at the end of this book. Your story can be one you have heard before, actual events, or a story you make up. Number each block of your story.

Additional Resources

Books

Harriet Powers

- *Sewing Stories: Harriet Powers' Journey from Slave to Artist* by Barbara Herkert and Vanessa Brantley-Newton

Slavery

- *Almost to Freedom* by Vaunda Micheaux Nelson, Colin Bootman
- *Aunt Harriet's Underground Railroad in the Sky* by Faith Ringgold
- *Love Twelve Miles Long* by Glenda Armand
- *Mumbet's Declaration of Independence* by Gretchen Woelfle
- *Show Way* by Jacqueline Woodson
- *Biddy Mason Speaks Up* by By Arisa White, Laura Atkins, Laura Freeman
- *Calico Girl* by Jerdine Nolen
- *Let It Shine: Stories of Black Women Freedom Fighters* By Andrea Davis Pinkney, Stephen Alcorn, Stephen Alcorn
- *The Women Who Caught The Babies* By Eloise Greenfield
- *Growing Up in Slavery: Stories of Young Slaves as Told by Themselves* By Yuval Taylor, Kathleen Judge

Videos

- Reading of *Sewing Stories*: https://www.youtube.com/watch?v=sr-ZJFUm2wk
- The Breathtaking Courage of Harriet Tubman: https://www.youtube.com/watch?v=Dv7YhVKFqbQ
- Why Did Europeans Enslave Africans?: https://www.youtube.com/watch?v=opUDFaqNgXc
- The Oral Tradition of Storytelling: https://www.youtube.com/watch?v=BNY7L_RdObA

Websites

- How white women's "investment" in slavery has shaped America today: https://www.vox.com/2019/8/19/20807633/slavery-white-women-stephanie-jones-rogers-1619
- Ways to Teach Kids About Slavery: https://www.tolerance.org/the-moment/december-10-2019-appropriate-ways-to-teach-kids-about-slavery
- Biography of Harriet Tubman: https://www.biography.com/activist/harriet-tubman

Lesson 2

The Bible Quilt

Harriet created her Bible Quilt, originally called Adam and Eve, in 1886. She put it on display at the Clark County Cotton Fair. An artist and teacher, Jennie Smith, saw the quilt there and wanted to buy it. Harriet was not ready to part with her quilt. 5 years later, because of financial difficulties, Harriet needed to sell the quilt. She went to Jennie Smith and asked for $10 in exchange for the quilt. Jennie only had $5 and Harriet reluctantly agreed to sell her the quilt. Harriet gave Jennie a description of each block, which Jennie wrote down and saved. Harriet returned several times to visit her quilt.

Bible Quilt Descriptions

FIRST ROW:

1. Adam and Eve in the Garden of Eden.

2. Continuance of Paradise with Eve and a son.

3. Satan amidst the seven stars [angels].

SECOND ROW:

1. Cain killing his brother Abel.

2. Cain goes into the land of Nod to get a wife.

3. Jacob's dream.

4. The baptism of Christ.

THIRD ROW:

1. The crucifixion.

2. Judas Iscariot and the thirty pieces of silver.

3. The Last Supper.

4. The Holy Family.

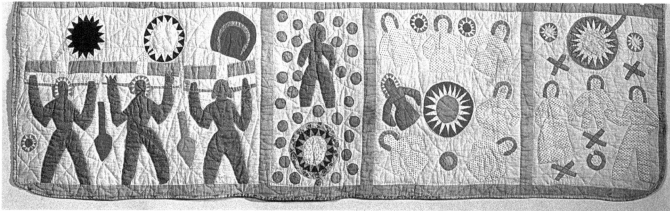

Examining the Artwork

Spend some time examining the work. Have the children write or tell you 5 things they notice about the artwork (optional journal pages are found at the end of the book). If they get stuck, try asking: What is going on? What do you see that makes you think that? What more can you find? Try not to ask questions that are too specific or give them any answers, let the observations be their own. Experience creates more lasting memories. It may take a while before they can look closely and come up with observations on their own, or are comfortable sharing them. After they have made their own observations, you can use the optional vocabulary and discussion questions below to look deeper.

Vocabulary

1. Shape- a 2-dimensional enclosed space, has length and width, can be geometric (like squares and circles) or organic (an irregular shape like a fried egg or a torn edge). Does this block use geometric or organic shapes?
2. Texture- describes the feel of a surface, it can be real (you could feel it with your hand) or implied (only looks like it feels bumpy, rough, silky, etc). What do you think this quilt feels like? If you were to examine this quilt in person, do you think it has a real or implied texture?
3. Movement- directing the viewer's eye around the piece or creating an illusion of action. Do elements create movement in this block? How does your eye want to move around this block: follow a path, jump around, etc.?
4. Quilt block- the units that are repeated to make up a quilt, usually squares. They can be a solid piece or made up of multiple pieces sewn together or appliquéd.
5. Illustrate- to make pictures to tell a story.
6. Storyboard- a series of sketches to show how a story will be illustrated, such as scenes in a movie.

Art in Action

If this block had sound effects, what would they sound like? Act them out.

Time To Create: Illustrate your Story

Materials:

- 'Illustrate Your Storyboard' from the journal at the back of this book (choose the one that matches your writing template)
- Large sheets of paper (if you do not enlarge the storyboard)
- Pencil
- Colored pencils or markers

In this lesson, you will be illustrating your story on the storyboard you started in the last lesson.

Decide how big you want your finished quilt to be. Enlarge copies of your storyboard or use a grid to draw it larger on the large sheets of paper. You can do 1 block per sheet of paper to make it easier to work with. Make sure the blocks are enlarged the same amount and still fit together.

Illustrate the story you wrote in the last lesson in each enlarged block. This is just a sketch to create the layout of shapes and colors for your quilt. Try to use simple, chunky shapes to make it easier to create appliqués in the next lesson.

Color or label each shape in your enlarged sketches. Number each shape to correspond to the numbered blocks of your story. Take a photo of the finished blocks laid out the way they will be in the finished quilt to refer back to later.

Additional Resources

Books

Harriet Powers

- *Stitching Stars: The Story Quilts of Harriet Powers (African-American Artists and Artisans)* by Mary E. Lyons

Quilts and Slavery

- *The Patchwork Path: A Quilt Map to Freedom* by Bettye Stroud and Erin Susanne Bennett
- *Hidden in Plain View: A Secret Story of Quilts and the Underground Railroad* by Jacqueline L. Tobin, Raymond G. Dobard, et al.
- *The Secret to Freedom* by Marcia Vaughan and Larry Johnson
- *Sweet Clara and the Freedom Quilt (Reading Rainbow Books)* by Deborah Hopkinson
- *The Quilt Code* by Margaret Turner Taylor
- *Harriet Tubman and My Grandmother's Quilts (African American Quartet)* by Lorenzo Pace

Videos

- What is a Storyboard: https://www.youtube.com/watch?v=BzxmGy80L_g
- African American Quilt Making Tradition: https://www.youtube.com/watch?v=ehTSQdwbeyg
- Quilts Underground: https://www.youtube.com/watch?v=PKFtJ_ZqfMY

Websites

- Smithsonian National Museum of American History (Bible Quilt): https://americanhistory.si.edu/collections/search/object/nmah_556462

Lesson 3

History of Quilts

This sculpture, the Ivory King, is from the Temple of Osiris in Abydos, Egypt dating as far back as 5000 years ago depicting a quilted cloak.

Quilted clothing was used under armor in 12th Century England. Bed quilts have been mentioned in 15th Century England, however, we don't know how they looked or were made as none have survived.

The Tristan Quilt is one of the earliest surviving examples of a decorative quilt in the world. Made in the 14th Century in Sicily, it is now in pieces. You can see sections in the London V&A Museum and the Florence Bargello Palace.

Throughout history, quilts were usually utilitarian, for warmth or protection. They were often made from scraps of old clothing, blankets, or worn quilts. Quilts made of new materials, sometimes expensive, and decorative quilts did also exist. While quilts were a necessity for the poor, who had to use and reuse everything available to them, noblewomen and upper-class women also made quilts. Today most quilts are sewn by machine using new materials, though hand sewing or recycled materials are used as well.

Anonymous, Caraco jacket in printed cotton, England, 1770-1790, skirt in quilted silk satin, 1750-1790.

Types of Quilts

1. Wholecloth Quilt- made of a single fabric with the design stitched on. The Tristan Quilt and quilted satin skirt are wholecloth quilts.

2. Appliqué Quilt- made up of background fabric with pieces of fabric attached on top. Harriet's quilts are applique.

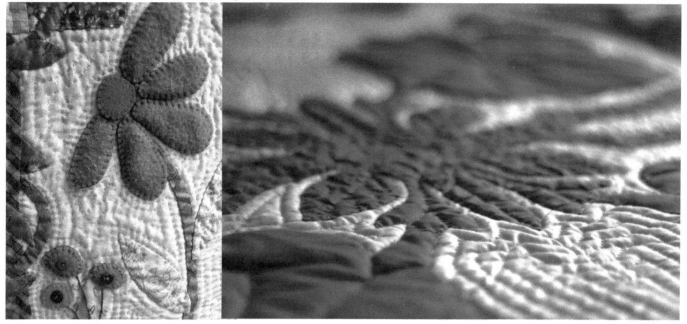

3. Pieced or Patchwork Quilt- made up of many pieces of fabric sewn together at their edges.

A Gallery of Our Own: Women of Art History

Examining the Artwork

Spend some time examining the work. Have the children write or tell you 5 things they notice about the artwork (optional journal pages are found at the end of the book). If they get stuck, try asking: What is going on? What do you see that makes you think that? What more can you find? Try not to ask questions that are too specific or give them any answers, let the observations be their own. Experience creates more lasting memories. It may take a while before they can look closely and come up with observations on their own, or are comfortable sharing them. After they have made their own observations, you can use the optional vocabulary and discussion questions below to look deeper.

Vocabulary

1. Balance- arranging the elements to distribute the visual weight in a pleasing way. Does this composition look balanced? Why or why not?
2. Rhythm- Arranging elements to repeat or alternate to create movement or cohesion. How does your eye move around the piece? Does it look cohesive?
3. Composition- the way the elements are placed in a piece. Does this piece have a pleasing composition?
4. Appliqué- (verb) to sew a piece of fabric onto a larger piece of fabric as decoration.
5. Quilt- (verb) to stitch through layers of cloth (and sometimes filler like batting) in a pattern, used to hold the layers together in a decorative way.
6. Seam allowance- the distance between the raw edge and the seam line. The seam allowance is usually 1/4" in quilting. The seam line is the line where you sew.

Art in Action

If this block were music, what would it sound like? Create a dance to go with the music and the block.

Time To Create: Quilt Blocks

Materials:

- Your illustrated storyboard from the last lesson
- Fabric (plain background fabric and colors to make your appliqués, I recommend knits like old t-shirts for the appliqué fabric for beginners)
- Disappearing fabric marker
- Straight pins, safety pins, or small weights
- Needle and thread
- Permanent fabric markers, fabric paint, or acrylic paint and fabric medium
- Cardboard
- Iron
- Freezer paper (optional for advanced students)
- Paper scissors
- Fabric scissors (if you have separate fabric scissors, otherwise any sharp scissors will do)
- Embroidery hoop (optional)
- Fabric glue (optional)
- Embroidery floss and embroidery needle (optional)

You will first need to decide if you will be making an appliquéd quilt like Harriet or a painted quilt like Faith Ringgold (see her later work on her website in the additional resources). Younger students may do best with a painted quilt, appliquéd with knit fabrics for intermediate, and appliquéd with woven fabrics for advanced students.

All Levels:

If you are using new fabric wash, dry, and iron it before starting. Pin each block to the background fabric, or use weights. Draw around the blocks with the disappearing fabric marker. Cut out the background fabric blocks and unpin the paper.

Beginner:

Trace the enlarged storyboard images onto the blocks. You can do this by taping them to a window with the storyboard in the back and drawing with the disappearing fabric marker. Tape or pin the blocks to cardboard to keep them still and flat, and to keep the paint from bleeding through onto the table. Paint or color the images on the blocks.

Intermediate:

Using paper scissors, cut out the shapes in your enlarged storyboard.

Pin your shapes to the knit fabrics you have chosen (or use weights to hold them down) and draw around each shape with the disappearing fabric marker.

Cut out the fabric shapes along the outer lines. The larger, chunkier shapes can be cut from fabric, but you can use fabric markers to fill in details later.

Lay your fabric shapes out on the background fabric blocks, use your photo as a reference for the layout. Pin or glue the shapes in place.

Hand or machine sew around the edges of each piece of fabric to securely attach them to the background blocks. If you are hand sewing, you may need to place the background fabric in an embroidery hoop to keep the stitches from bunching up the fabric as you sew.

Use permanent fabric markers or paint to fill in the details on each block. Iron the finished blocks flat and heat set the marker. Be careful not to melt any acrylic paint you may have used.

Advanced:

Trace each shape onto freezer paper and cut them out.

Iron the freezer paper shapes onto the colored fabric, the waxy side toward the fabric. Cut out the shape, leaving ⅛-¼ inch outside of the freezer paper. That will be the part that gets folded under to hide the raw edges.

Peel the freezer paper off and place it on the back of the shape, waxy side up. Carefully fold over and iron the extra fabric to the freezer paper.

Arrange your shapes on the background fabric and iron the freezer paper in a small place on each side to hold it in place, or use a few small dots of fabric glue.

Hand or machine stitch around each shape, use thread that matches the fabric if you can.

Once all the shapes are sewn, carefully cut a hole in the back behind each shape (leave at least ¼" of fabric between the hole and the stitches). Carefully pull the freezer paper out of the hole.

Fill in the details using the permanent fabric markers or embroidery. If using embroidery, use an embroidery hoop to hold the fabric taught. Iron the blocks flat and set them aside.

Additional Resources

Books

Quilts
- *The Quilt* by Ann Jonas
- *The Keeping Quilt* by Patricia Polacco
- *The Quiltmaker's Gift* by Jeff Brumbeau
- *The Josefina Story Quilt* by Eleanor Coerr
- *Tar Beach* by Faith Ringgold
- *With Needle and Thread: A Book about Quilts* by Raymond Bial

Videos

- The History of Quilting: https://www.youtube.com/watch?v=CEFPJb9HqKA
- Appliqué Tutorial- Freezer Paper Method: https://www.youtube.com/watch?v=Ljl_O2aOT1M
- Hand Embroidery for Beginners: https://www.youtube.com/watch?v=kKnBUa4l2k4

Websites

- Complete list of Common Quilting Terms: https://www.allpeoplequilt.com/how-to-quilt/quilting-basics/complete-list-common-quilting-terms
- Faith Ringgold: https://www.faithringgold.com/

Materials

You can get bundles of small pieces of coordinating fabrics from Walmart, Amazon, crafts or fabric stores, Tuesday Morning, or sometimes even a dollar store. Old clothes are also a good source of fabric. Old t-shirts, fleece, or felt work well for beginners because the edges don't fray, so will not need to be turned under.

You want a sturdy woven fabric for the background in a solid, neutral color so it doesn't distract from the images. Old sheets or quilters cotton work well.

Fabric markers, fabric paint, fabric medium, and disappearing fabric markers can be found at craft stores or fabric stores.

Lesson 4

What makes Harriet's Quilts Special

It is very unusual to find such detailed descriptions from the artist of any artwork, much less a quilt. Harriet left us great insight into her life and art.

Abomey Appliqué

Her bold shapes and technique were very much like Abomey appliqué and Impressionism.

On the Beach by French Impressionist painter Léon Pourtau 1872-1898

The bible quilt is made up of 299 fabric pieces, with bright colors and different textures. The blocks are uneven shapes and sizes and are separated by broken sashing. The great care and time put into these quilts tell how important they were to Harriet.

Dahomey Kingdom

Abomey Appliqué originated in the Dahomey Kingdom, in modern-day Benin in West Africa. The Dahomey Kingdom existed from 1600 to 1904. The appliqué technique was likely invented by the Fon people living in Abomey, the capital. The appliqués depicted the deeds and assumed names of the Fon royalty. They were also given as gifts to warriors and chiefs to commemorate their achievements and to allied nations. The appliqués symbolized power and status.

The Dahomey Kingdom was home to the only consistently deployed force of women warriors in the world at the time, called Mino or "our mothers". They were fierce fighters. They trained by climbing through acacia thorns, wrestling, survival training alone in the wilderness for up to 9 days with minimal rations, and throwing prisoners from the walls. They rewarded the bravest with belts of thorns. They also served as royal bodyguards.

Dahomey Mino with the King 1890

Harriet Powers

Dahomey was the last African kingdom to fall to European colonization, and was invaded by France. It regained its independence in 1960 and was renamed Benin in 1975. The last known Dahomey Mino, Nawi, died in 1979, at well over 100 years old.

Europeans called the Mino Amazons. The Amazons were a group of female warriors in Greek legends.

A Amazon in the Dahomey Army by Frederick Edwyn Forbes 1851

Dahomey Mino officers. The horns, probably made of tin, are insignia of rank.

Examining the Artwork

Spend some time examining the work. Have the children write or tell you 5 things they notice about the artwork (optional journal pages are found at the end of the book). If they get stuck, try asking: What is going on? What do you see that makes you think that? What more can you find? Try not to ask questions that are too specific or give them any answers, let the observations be their own. Experience creates more lasting memories. It may take a while before they can look closely and come up with observations on their own, or are comfortable sharing them. After they have made their own observations, you can use the optional vocabulary and discussion questions below to look deeper.

Vocabulary

1. Color- produced when light strikes an object and reflects back to the eye. The properties of color are hue, value, and intensity.
   What are the colors like in this piece? (bright, muted, monochromatic, similar, different, earthy, etc)
2. Hue- blue, red, yellow, cerulean, taupe, etc.
   How many different hues can you find in this block?
3. Value- lightness or darkness, made by adding black or white to a hue
   Where is a lighter value used? Where is a darker value used?
4. Intensity- how bright the color is.
   Which colors in this block have the most intensity? Which colors have the least intensity?
5. Impressionism: an art movement that works to capture an impression of a moment in time.
6. Sashing: Strips of fabric between each block to separate or enhance the blocks.

Art in Action

Look at the artwork from really close, then really far. Put your face right on the left side and then the right. How does the artwork look when you see it from different positions?

Time To Create: Assemble Your Quilt

Now it is time to decide if you want sashing or if you want the blocks to be sewn straight to each other.

Quilt with sashing.   Quilt without sashing.

Materials:

- Finished quilt blocks
- 1-2 fabrics for sashing, if you choose to use it
- Iron
- Sewing machine or needle and thread
- Sharp scissors
- Ruler

These videos show how to sew the quilt blocks together without sashing.

- Sewing squares together: https://www.youtube.com/watch?v=hkYkGO8xMgc
- Sewing Rows Together: https://www.youtube.com/watch?v=nwlSZjq7Arg

These videos show how to make sashing.

- Quilt Sashing Lesson #1: https://www.youtube.com/watch?v=qcIAh8hvgAo
- Quilt Sashing Lesson #2: https://www.youtube.com/watch?v=M6oR72dNCXY

Additional Resources

Books

- *The Name Quilt* by Phyllis Root
- *Stitchin' and Pullin': A Gee's Bend Quilt* by Patricia C. McKissack
- *Pieces: A Year in Poems Quilts* by Anna Grossnickle Hines
- *The Canada Geese Quilt* by Natalie Kinsey-Warnock and Leslie W. Bowman
- *Quilting Now & Then* by Karen B. Willing, Julie B. Dock, Sarah Morse

Videos

- The Origin Of The Dahomey Amazons: https://www.youtube.com/watch?v=pKzLQmSIBNU
- Story quilts by Rumi OBrien: https://www.youtube.com/watch?v=xqFze15cweQ

Websites

- Palace Sculptures of Abomey: http://d2aohiyo3d3idm.cloudfront.net/publications/virtuallibrary/0892365692.pdf

Lesson 5

Harriet's Later Life

Jennie Smith displayed the Bible Quilt at the Exposition in Atlanta in 1896, where Harriet saw it the day after Christmas. December 26th was the day that black people were allowed to attend the Exposition and there was a reported attendance of 30,000 people. There was a parade of black military troops, recitations, speeches, music, crafts, and art displays.

Harriet's family encountered financial difficulties in the 1890s and they sold off parts of the farm. Her husband left in 1895. The little we know about Harriet's life is thanks to the letters she wrote and the records kept by the women who purchased her quilts. The date of Harriet's death, Jan. 1, 1910, was recently discovered on her gravestone in Athen's Gospel Pilgrim Cemetery.

10630. The Nursery, Atlanta Exposition.

Harriet wrote the following letter to Lorene Divers, one of the women who wanted to buy the Bible Quilt:

Athens, GA

Jan 28th, 1896

The life of Harriet Powers. Born in Madison Co. 8 miles from Athens on the Elberton Road in the year Oct. 29, 1837. Her mistress was Nancy Lester. I commenced to learn at 11 years old and the white children learn me by sound on a poplar leaf. On Sundays after that I on books and done my own studying. I was married to Armsted Powers 1855. When I was free I moved to Dondy, Ga. In 1872 I made a quilt of 4 thousand and 50 diamonds.

In 1886 we moved to Athens and in 1887 I represented the star quilt in the colored fair association of Athens — Mr. Madison Davis, Pres, E. W. Bridy, clerk. The quit of mine taken the premium.

In 1882 I became a member of the Mt. Zion Baptist church. Then I visited Sunday school and read the Bible more than ever. Then I composed a quilt of the Lord's Supper from the New Testament. 2 thousand and 500 diamonds.

In the year 1888, I composed and completed the quilt of Adam And Eve in the Garden of Eden—afterward sold it to Miss. Jennie Smith, and it was represented by her at the Exposition in Atlanta. I was there at the Ex — Dec. 26, 1896.

I am the mother of 9 children—6 dead and 3 living. I am 58 years old.

After leaving Atlanta it was said that I was dead—it was not so, for I was at the Exposition because I present the Governor of the colored department a watermelon Christmas gift. I am enjoying good health in Athens, Ga.

This I accomplish

Harriet Powers

Storytelling

Storytelling has always been an important way to pass on traditions and history. From cave paintings made over 30,000 years ago to the movies and books of today, storytelling preserves history, imparts morality or caution, and entertains. Murals carved or painted on walls, myths or legends passed down orally, fairy tales, plays, newspapers, art, and even music are forms of storytelling.

10,000 year old Bhimbetka cave paintings.

Stories can be about real events (factual or nonfiction) or made up (fiction). Harriet's quilts tell many stories, a different one in each block. Faith Ringgold's quilts tell a single story in each quilt.

Examining the Artwork

Spend some time examining the work. Have the children write or tell you 5 things they notice about the artwork (optional journal pages are found at the end of the book). If they get stuck, try asking: What is going on? What do you see that makes you think that? What more can you find? Try not to ask questions that are too specific or give them any answers, let the observations be their own. Experience creates more lasting memories. It may take a while before they can look closely and come up with observations on their own, or are comfortable sharing them. After they have made their own observations, you can use the optional vocabulary and discussion questions below to look deeper.

Vocabulary

1. Emphasis- using elements to emphasize a part of the artwork, such as a focal point. Where is the emphasis in this artwork? What draws your eye to that place? Do you think the artist intended to emphasize that place?
2. Repetition- an element (such as a shape, form, or color) is used over and over to create a pattern.
   Do you see any repetition in this piece? Does it make a pattern?
3. Harmony- parts of the composition are similar or repeated to bring it together and create balance.
   What elements are repeated? Does repetition make this piece look cohesive and balanced?
4. Fiction- writing about imaginary people, places, or events. Fiction can also include real people, places, or events, but makes up a story about them.
5. Nonfiction- writing about facts: real people, places, and events.
6. Self-binding- wrapping the fabric from the back of the quilt around to the front as the binding.

Art in Action

Spend 5 minutes looking at this quilt block. Turn away or cover the artwork and draw everything you remember. How much did you remember? What did you forget?

Time To Create: Assembling a Quilt Part 2

Materials:

- Fabric for borders (optional)
- Quilt batting or an old fleece blanket several inches larger than your finished quilt top, including borders
- Solid piece of fabric several inches larger than your quilt top, including borders (you can use a fleece blanket as both the filling layer and backing if you want a thinner quilt)
- Safety pins
- Sharp scissors
- Iron
- Sewing machine or needle and thread

This video shows how to add borders and backing. We will save the squaring up, quilting, and binding portions for the next lesson: https://www.youtube.com/watch?v=SE5CqpWaReA

Decide if you want borders around your quilt block. If so, add them now. Make your quilt sandwich (layer the backing facing down, then your batting, and finally your quilt top facing up). Make sure your layers are all even, centered, smooth, and pinned together.

Additional Resources

Books

Quilts
- *The Patchwork Quilt* by Valerie Flournoy
- *Luka's Quilt* by Georgia Guback
- *The Quilt Story* by Tony Johnston
- *The Tamale Quilt: Story Recipe Quilt Pattern* by Jane Tenorio-Coscarelli
- *The Tortilla Quilt Story Hardcover* by Jane Tenorio-Coscarelli

Faith Ringgold
- *Faith Ringgold: A View from the Studio* by Faith Ringgold and Curlee Raven Holton
- *Talking to Faith Ringgold* by Faith Ringgold

Storytelling
- *Mira and the Big Story* by Laura Alary & illustrated by Sue Todd
- *Ta-Da! Written* by Kathy Ellen Davis & illustrated by Kaylani Juanita
- *The Panda Problem* by Deborah Underwood
- *The Story Web* by Megan Frazer Blakemore
- *Tea Cakes for Tosh* by Kelly Starling Lyons & illustrated by E. B. Lewis

Videos
- Artist Faith Ringgold talks about the process of creating the Tar Beach story quilt: https://www.youtube.com/watch?v=794M-mcOJY4

Lesson 6

The Pictorial Quilt

A group of faculty wives or female faculty members from Atlanta University commissioned the pictorial quilt as a gift for Dr. Charles Cuthbert Hall. They presented the quilt to him in 1898.

The doctor's son, Reverend Basil Hall, tried to sell the quilt to the Museum of Fine Arts in Boston. The museum thought it would be more prestigious if the quilt were donated by a collector, so the Reverend sold the quilt to Maxim Karolik, a folk art collector. He later donated it to the museum.

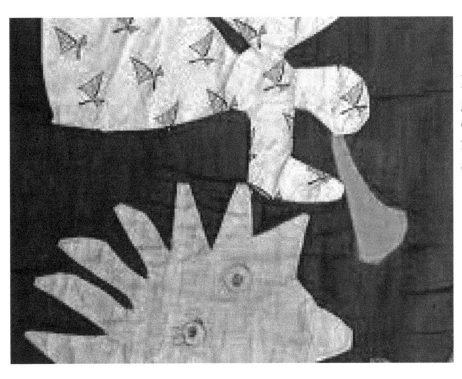

Robert Utter, the great-grandson of Charles Hall, drew eyes on some of the figures with a ballpoint pen as a child.

Harriet Powers

Pictorial Quilt Descriptions

FIRST ROW:

1. Job praying for his enemies. Job crosses. Job's coffin.

2. The dark day of May 19, 1780. The seven stars were seen 12 N. in the day. The cattle wall went to bed, chickens to roost and the trumpet was blown. The sun went off to a small spot and then to darkness.

3. The serpent lifted up by Moses and women bringing their children to look upon it to be healed.

4. Adam and Eve in the garden. Eve tempted by the serpent. Adam's rib by which Eve was made. The sun and the moon. God's all-seeing eye and God's merciful hand.

5. John baptizing Christ and the spirit of God descending and resting upon his shoulder like a dove.

SECOND ROW:

1. Jonah cast over board of the ship and swallowed by a whale. Turtles.

2. God created two of every kind, male and female.

3. The falling of the stars on Nov. 13, 1833. The people were frightened and thought that the end had come. God's hand staid the stars. The varmints rushed out of their beds.

4. Two of every kind of animal continued...camels, elephants, "gheraffs," lions, etc.

A Gallery of Our Own: Women of Art History

5. The angels of wrath and the seven vials. The blood of fornications. Seven-headed beast and 10 horns which arose of the water.

THIRD ROW:

1. Cold Thursday, 10 of February, 1895. A woman frozen while at prayer. A woman frozen at a gateway. A man with a sack of meal frozen. Icicles formed from the breath of a mule. All blue birds killed. A man frozen at his jug of liquor.

2. The red light night of 1846. A man tolling the bell to notify the people of the wonder. Women, children and fowls frightened by God's merciful hand caused no harm to them.

3. Rich people who were taught nothing of God. Bob Johnson and Kate Bell of Virginia. They told their parents to stop the clock at one and tomorrow it would strike one and so it did. This was the signal that they had entered everlasting punishment. The independent hog which ran 500 miles from Georgia to Virginia, her name was Betts.

4. The creation of animals continues.

5. The crucifixion of Christ between the two thieves. The sun went into darkness. Mary and Martha weeping at his feet. The blood and water run from his right side.

Harriet Powers

Spend some time examining the work. Have the children write or tell you 5 things they notice about the artwork (optional journal pages are found at the end of the book). If they get stuck, try asking: What is going on? What do you see that makes you think that? What more can you find? Try not to ask questions that are too specific or give them any answers, instead let the observations be their own. Experience creates more lasting memories. It may take a while before they can look closely and come up with observations on their own, or are comfortable sharing them. After they have made their own observations, you can use the optional vocabulary and discussion questions below to look deeper.

Vocabulary

1. Space- the areas around, within, or between the parts of a piece. Space is positive (such as an object)or negative (such as the space around an object), 2D or 3D. It can create an illusion of depth, make an area look open or closed.
   Does the space look open or closed? 2D or 3D?
2. Variety- putting together elements to add interest or a focal point, such as straight lines and curves, 2D and 3D, different sizes or colors or forms.
   How did the artist use variety in this piece? Does it make the quilt more interesting? How?
3. Unity- the elements in a piece work together to create a sense of wholeness.
   What elements are repeated? How do they work together? Does the quilt look unified?
4. Stitch-in-the-ditch quilting- sewing in the seams to define blocks or accentuate shapes.
5. Lap quilting- quilting by hand in the lap without a hoop.
6. Tableaux vivant- real-life recreations of artwork, also known as living pictures.

Art in Action

Create a tableaux vivant. Use your body, props, and objects from around the house to recreate the scenes in this quilt.

Time To Create: Quilting

Materials:

- Blanket binding, double-fold bias tape, or fabric (if you are not doing self-binding)
- Water-soluble fabric glue stick
- Straight edge or yardstick
- Sharp scissors
- Iron
- Sewing machine or needle and thread
- Yarn (optional)

Quilting is necessary to keep the layers together and straight. Some types of batting will come apart in the wash if the quilt is not quilted. Here are several easy quilting methods:

Hand Tie a Quilt (I recommend this method for beginners):

https://www.youtube.com/watch?v=GYTRL9YeUUs&list=PL233wsmULhHhqdLfu7Eg5eJDXuZQEfxNp&index=48

Hand Quilting:

https://www.youtube.com/watch?v=8DXN5Ger_jo

Machine Quilting:

https://www.youtube.com/watch?v=R7EdVJailUQ&list=PL233wsmULhHhqdLfu7Eg5eJDXuZQEfxNp&index=42

This video shows how to self-bind your quilt:

https://www.youtube.com/watch?v=6aXN-vjv4hA

Choose one of the above quilting methods and quilt the entire project. Square up your quilt using the straight edge, making sure you don't cut through the backing if you choose self-binding. Choose one of the binding methods from the video in the last lesson and follow the directions to bind your quilt.

Additional Resources

Books

- *The Pinata Quilt Hardcover* by Jane Tenorio-Coscarelli
- *I Lay My Stitches Down* by Cynthia Grady
- *The Quilt That Wouldn't Quit* by Cynthia Gibson
- *If Quilts Could Talk: My Quilts, My Stories Volume 1* by Aisha Lumumba
- *Victoria's Quilt Remembered* by Dorothy J. Dixon

References

- New Georgia Encyclopedia: https://www.georgiaencyclopedia.org/articles/arts-culture/harriet-powers-1837-1910
- Georgia Women of Achievement: https://www.georgiawomen.org/copy-of-pauley-frances-freeborn
- Museum of Fine Arts Boston https://collections.mfa.org/objects/116166
- National Museum of American History Behring Center: https://americanhistory.si.edu/collections/search/object/nmah_556462
- The Clarion (Spring 1982): https://issuu.com/american_folk_art_museum/docs/clarion_spr1982
- Quilting in America: https://www.quilting-in-america.com/History-of-Quilts.html
- The Spruce Crafts: https://www.thesprucecrafts.com/applique-in-quilts-2821555#:~:text=Applique%20is%20a%20term%20that,used%20to%20cut%20the%20patches.
- Biography of Harriet Tubman: https://www.biography.com/activist/harriet-tubman
- Abomey Appliqué: https://tdsblog.com/abomey-applique/
- Historical Museum of Abomey: http://www.epa-prema.net/abomeyGB/resources/hangings.htm#
- Smithsonian Magazine: https://www.smithsonianmag.com/history/dahomeys-women-warriors-88286072/
- Harriet Powers and the Power of Quilts | THE FÁBRICA: https://thefabrica.org/harriet-powers-and-the-power-of-quilts/

Image Credits

- Nana by Melanie Baxter
- Maps of Georgia by Melanie Baxter
- Child Reading the Bible by Free-Photos from Pixabay
- Child-4617142 by Manuela Milani from Pixabay
- Power-5508643 Image by Redleaf_Lodi from Pixabay
- Brookes slave ship, British Library: https://commons.wikimedia.org/wiki/File:Brookes_slave_ship,_British_Library.jpg
- Oak Alley Plantation by USA-Reiseblogger from Pixabay
- Slave Quarters by Dennis Larsen from Pixabay
- Harriet Tubman: https://commons.wikimedia.org/wiki/File:Carte-de-visite_portrait_of_Harriet_Tubman.jpg
- Emancipation Proclamation: https://commons.wikimedia.org/wiki/File:Emancipation_Proclamation.jpg
- Nocturne in Rosa und Grau, Porträt der Lady Meux: https://commons.wikimedia.org/wiki/File:James_Abbot_McNeill_Whistler_011.jpg
- Bible Quilt: https://commons.wikimedia.org/wiki/File:PowersBibleQuilt_1886.jpg
- Pictorial Quilt: https://commons.wikimedia.org/wiki/File:PowersBibleQuilt_1898.jpg

- Statue Ivory King Petrie: https://commons.wikimedia.org/wiki/File:Statue_ivory_king_Petrie.jpg
- Tristan Quilt: https://commons.wikimedia.org/wiki/File:Le_Tristan_quilt_Noble_et_son_h%C3%A9rault_1395.jpg
- 18th Century Dress: https://commons.wikimedia.org/wiki/File:Caraco_jacket_in_printed_cotton,_1770-1790,_skirt_in_quilted_silk_satin,_1750-1790.jpg
- Wholecloth Quilt 1: https://commons.wikimedia.org/wiki/File:Wholecloth_quilt_MET_DP123110.jpg
- Wholecloth Quilt 2 by xiaoping606 from Pixabay
- Appliqué Quilt 1 by bego eguia from Pixabay
- Appliqué Quilt 2 by mching49 from Pixabay
- Pieced Quilt 1 by Candace Hunter from Pixabay
- Pieced Quilt 2 by pixel1 from Pixabay
- Harriet Powers: https://commons.wikimedia.org/wiki/File:Harriet_Powers_1901.png
- On the Beach: https://commons.wikimedia.org/wiki/File:L%C3%A9on_Pourteau_-_Sur_la_plage.jpg
- Abomey Appliqué: https://commons.wikimedia.org/wiki/File:Abomey-Tissus_appliqu%C3%A9s.jpg
- Map of Benin by Melanie Baxter
- Dahomey Mino 1: https://commons.wikimedia.org/wiki/File:Dahomey_amazon2.jpg
- Dahomey Mino 2: https://commons.wikimedia.org/wiki/File:Female_officers_amazons_in_Dahomey.png
- Dahomey Mino 3: https://commons.wikimedia.org/wiki/File:Seh-Dong-Hong-Be.jpg
- Quilt with Sashing by Eveline de Bruin from Pixabay
- Quilt without Sashing by Mark Martins from Pixabay
- The Nursery: https://commons.wikimedia.org/wiki/File:The_Nursery,_Atlanta_Exposition,_by_Kilburn,_B._W._(Benjamin_West),_1827-1909.jpg
- Bhimbetka Cave Paintings: https://commons.wikimedia.org/wiki/File:Bhimbetka_Cave_Paintings.jpg

HARRIET POWERS
Journal

_____
Artist's Name

Lived from _____ to _____

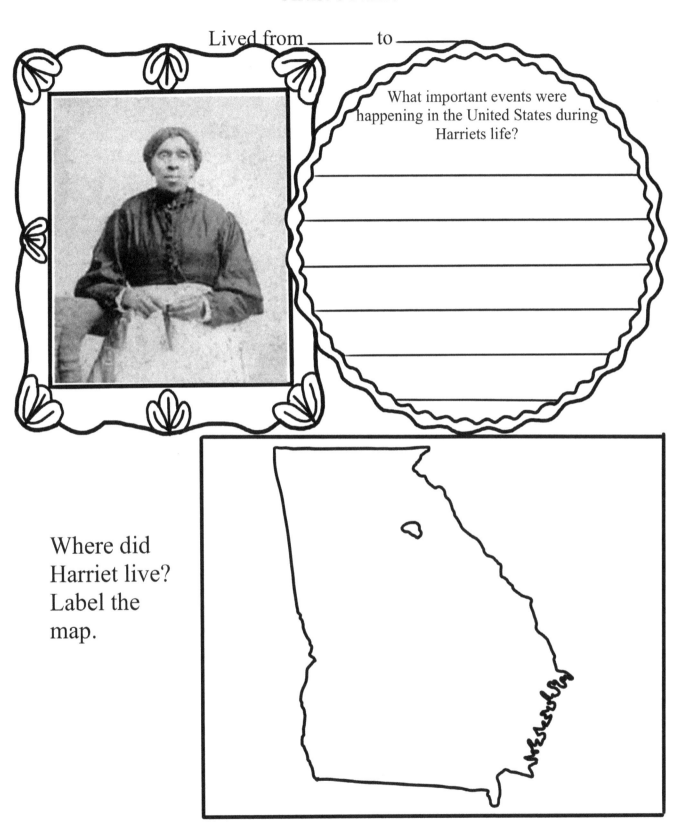

What important events were
happening in the United States during
Harriets life?

Where did
Harriet live?
Label the
map.

This artist's art makes me feel:

_____
_____
_____
_____
_____
_____
_____
_____

This artists's work was:
☐ 2 dimensional
☐ 3 dimensional
☐ Both
☐ Performance
☐ All of the above

This artist created with these materials:

_____
_____
_____
_____
_____
_____
_____

What makes this artist unique? struggles, innovation, style, etc.

_____
_____
_____
_____
_____
_____

Other interesting facts about this artist:

_____
_____
_____
_____
_____

What do I notice about this piece?

1._____

2._____

3._____

4._____

5._____

What do I notice about this piece?

1._____

2._____

3._____

4._____

5._____

What do I notice about this piece?

1._____

2._____

3._____

4._____

5._____

What do I notice about this piece?

1._____

2._____

3._____

4._____

5._____

What do I notice about this piece?

1._____

2._____

3._____

4._____

5._____

What do I notice about this piece?

1._____

2._____

3._____

4._____

5._____

Vocabulary

Elements of Art

These are the basic parts the artist uses to create aesthetically pleasing art.

1. Line:_____
   _____

2. Shape:_____
   _____

3. Color:_____
   _____

   a. Hue:_____
      _____

   b. Value:_____
      _____

   c. Intensity:_____
      _____

4. Form:_____
   _____

5. Texture:_____
   _____

6. Space:_____
   _____

Principles of Design

These are the ways an artist combines the elements of art.

1. Contrast:_____

    _____

2. Balance:_____

    _____

3. Emphasis:_____

    _____

4. Repetition:_____

    _____

5. Pattern:_____

    _____

6. Rhythm:_____

    _____

7. Movement:_____

    _____

8. Variety:_____

    _____

9. Proportion:_____

    _____

10. Harmony:_____

    _____

11. Unity:_____

    _____

Other Terms

1. Storyteller-_____
_____

2. Oral traditions-_____
_____

3. Quilt block-_____
_____

4. Illustrate-_____
_____

5. Storyboard-_____
_____

6. Appliqué (verb)-_____
_____

7. Quilt (verb)-_____
_____

8. Seam Allowance-_____
_____

9. Impressionism-_____
_____

10. Sashing-_____
_____

11. Fiction-_____
_____

12. Nonfiction-_____
_____

13. Self-binding-_____
_____

14. Stitch-in-the-ditch quilting-_____
_____

15. Lap Quilting-_____
_____

16. Tableaux vivant-_____
_____

Storyboard Templates

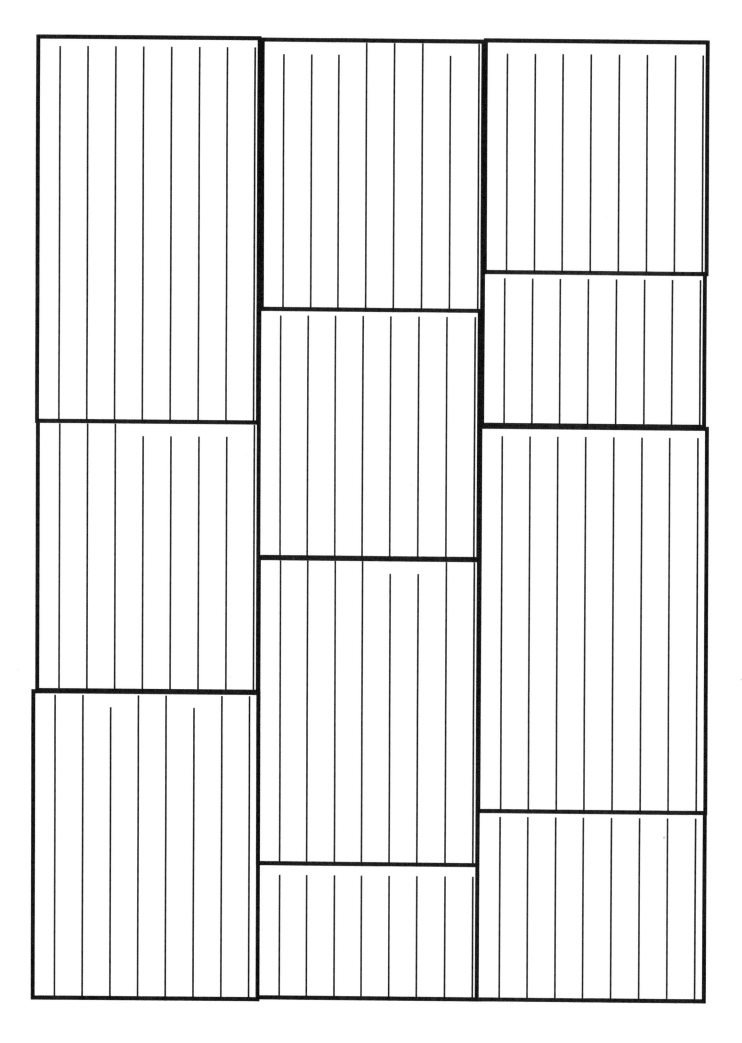